# Great Granny Margaret's Uber Diary

Margaret High

# Great Granny Margaret's Uber Diary

Copyright © 2019
Margaret High
Cambridge, Ontario
CANADA

Great Granny Margaret's Uber Diary

Copyright © 2019 by Margaret High
Book Cover Design & Typesetting by Becca Blue Studios
Published by Margaret High
Cambridge, Ontario, Canada

All rights reserved. This book is protected under the copyright laws of the United States of America and applicable international copyright treaties. No part of this book may be reproduced, stored in a retrieval system, or transmitted in any form or by any other means without prior written permission of the publisher. Reviewers and other writers are hereby granted permission to use brief quotations in articles and reviews, provided proper credit is given to the author and publisher.

To contact the author, please email:
margaretehigh@gmail.com

Facebook Page: @authormargarethigh

Printed in the United States of America
For Worldwide Distribution
ISBN 978-0-9809826-5-7

"No names or dates are given to protect the privacy of passengers. These are just my day to day observations and talks with some wonderful people from all over the world." - Margaret High

# Why I Decided To Drive For Uber

My Son suggested to me that I should be an Uber Driver. I thought he was joking. I had heard about Uber, but there was so much controversy, and the taxi drivers were up in arms. I surely didn't want to be on the receiving end of that.

It was April of 2016 and I had just celebrated my sixty-eighth Birthday. Being retired now and having so much time on my hands, my Son suggested the Uber driver idea. He knew I was a people person and figured it would be perfect for me—a great use for my spare time and a way to earn some side money. What would I have to lose? And if I didn't like it, I wasn't locked into anything—so I made up my mind to go for it. I was going to be an Uber driver.

I quickly downloaded the App on my phone and uploaded all the documentation needed to get started. I felt many different feelings in this moment. I felt anxious, nervous, and excited all at once. My biggest worry was still the Taxi drivers, but as it turned out, I had nothing to worry about. Uber was quickly accepted in our city and the people made it known that they wanted Uber too! So it became legal, and my new journey began.

# My First Day

Well, the first time I heard the sound on my phone, I panicked. A pop-up told me that I was to pickup a passenger at a certain address. My navigation system took me step by step to my pickup, and needless to say, I was very excited.

My first passenger turned out to be a student at a local college. He was originally from India and had just arrived this week.

"Wow! How do you like our winter?" I asked.

"Very cold," he replied, "I liked the snow when I first saw it, but I don't like the cold."

We both laughed.

This was a pleasant passenger on his way from school to his job. I felt good about my first day. The only problem I had was trying to figure out the navigation system. It wasn't cooperating very well, or maybe it was me? I think it was just a matter of getting used to it—I guess.

My first day was definitely busy, I was picking up students from the local colleges and universities. The amazing thing about being an Uber driver is that you are recognized by most of the students from all over the world. One student said it made him feel at home because Uber drivers are pretty well known where he was from. Some of the female passengers even commented that it was great to see a woman driver, and because I was a senior citizen they felt very comfortable with me.

# Learning My Way Around

It took some time for me to figure out the navigation system. In some areas it didn't recognize the address, or it would take me to a parking lot, or even say I've arrived—but it was in the middle of nowhere!

With time and updates, I found my navigation system was getting a little more accurate. I was learning to maneuver around the city pretty well, and for me, this was quite a challenge maneuvering through the construction on many of our streets. Before Uber, I would only drive to the places that I was familiar with. I knew this would be one of the many challenges I would have to overcome as an Uber driver moving forward. But going outside my comfort zone would help me become a better person and give me more confidence while driving. I was sure of it.

By this time, I was getting more excited to meet new people and to hear their stories. I loved to listen to my passengers talk about their homeland, family, and how they miss them. I quickly realized how tough it must be to come to a new school, a new country, and learn a different language. The sacrifice their parents and themselves must make just so their children could come to Canada and get educated—something I think we take for granted here.

I learned that young men from India really miss their mothers, their culture and the women who cook, clean, and do the laundry for the men—it's a big culture shock for them to do this for themselves!

# An Interesting Story

On the way to a very long trip out of the city, my passenger was telling me a story about a very good friend. She said that her friend was in prison for a long time and that she had a very interesting story to tell.

I didn't ask any personal questions such as why she was in prison, but my passenger did say that her friend left her country because her father was killed by the Mafia, and her friend's boyfriend was not a very nice man. She said it was a part of the reason why her friend was in prison.

I expressed my sympathy to her and her friend, then suggested that being an author myself, if her friend has a story to tell, that maybe she should consider writing a book about her experience.

"Funny you should say that," she said, "because that's exactly what she's doing."

"I'm sure it will be an interesting read." I replied.

She nodded, "I know it will."

Since then, I have often wondered if her friend did write that book, or at least started it.

# My First Drive to the Airport

I picked up a couple heading to the airport at 1:30 in the afternoon. Their flight was going out at 7:00pm that night. You'd think there would be lots of time because it's only an hour drive to the airport, but it wasn't the case that day.

Heavy traffic caused a bumper to bumper slowdown, and to make a long story short we didn't get to the airport until 6:30pm! Needless to say, my passengers were very upset on the ride in—worried they weren't going to make the flight. On the way, my passenger prayed to all the gods out there—all while I was trying to get there on time, but I couldn't control the traffic.

By the time I got there, I was a nervous wreck. It was the quickest drop-off and unloading of luggage that I've ever had. Lol.

But they made it—barely. At least, I hope they made it in time.

# Sometimes We Just Need Someone To Listen

Today I picked up a young passenger who seemed very stressed, and it looked like she had been crying. I asked her if she was alright.

"No," she replied.

"Oh, I'm sorry. Is there anything I can do?" I asked.

"No," she spoke again, "I just want to Die!"

Wow! That went straight to my heart. So young, and yet wanting to die. She went on to tell me that she was drinking all night trying to kill herself with alcohol. I could tell this passenger was in a lot of pain, so I asked her if she had someone to talk to?

"Yes, that's where I'm going now." She said.

I let her know that she wasn't alone and that there is help out there, but you have to want it. I told her about friends of mine having the same thoughts and feelings as she does right now. I then gave her the name of a place to call. She was very happy about the advice—that I even cared.

She told me her entire story and I listened without judging. She had a drug problem and most of her friends were all drug users, which made it hard for her to quit. She said that if she quit, she would lose her friends.

"All I have is my friends, my family has given up on me." She said.

I felt sorry for this young girl, having to go through such pain, so I had to be very careful with my response. I told her that I understand. I quickly saw relief in her eyes.

"Thank you so much for listening to me," she said.

"You are very welcome," I replied, "but there are a lot of people out there who do care, so please contact the place I mentioned so they can help you."

  At the end, I gave her a hug and wished her luck. I hope she got the help she so desperately needed. I often think about her. There truly is help out there, you can look it up on the Internet and it will direct you to the nearest help centre to your location. You are not alone!

# Thanks, But No Thanks

I was called to pick up two young men. When they first got into my car, I think I could smell liquor, but I wasn't sure—they confirmed it later. They wanted to be dropped off at a friend's house to continue partying.

"Why don't you come party with us?" They said.

I laughed, "I'm a Grandma and a Great-Grandma. You don't want me to party with you,"

"Sure, why not," they said. "You look good for being a Grandma. You seem to have lots of energy. I bet you could out party us!" One of them said.

"I am flattered, but no thanks," I replied. "You both are my Grandson's age, and I'm sure they wouldn't want me to go to a party with their friends either."

They were definitely drunk, so I took it as a joke and laughed it off. I'm sure once the young men sobered up and came to their senses, they'll feel a little embarrassed for their words—if they remember them.

Thankfully, with all my Ubering, I have never felt in danger or uncomfortable. I guess it's how I look at things. I figure, if I treat people with respect, I will get respect back—and it's always good to have a sense of humour.

Later on that day, I met two awesome women. One of the young women was from India, and was only in Canada for a few months. I was very impressed with how good her English was. She was telling me that this was her first winter here and she wasn't prepared for the cold.

I told her, "I live here, and I'm never prepared for the cold."
We both laughed.

The other woman that day was a senior. She had called Uber because she was in a car accident and was injured. She said that she didn't have her car anymore.

"I'm glad you are here and OK," I said, "except for the injured foot. It seems you were very lucky."

She agreed, then went on to tell me that she had worked as a Librarian for many years and she loved to read. I immediately wondered how many books she would be reading now that she couldn't drive anymore?

The next pickup was a young student who was very pleasant. He talked about his business as a DJ (Disc Jockey), which he does with a friend. They had started a small business and were getting very busy. With going to college and earning an income, he was very much an entrepreneur. I congratulated him and took his business card. I said I will pass it on if I met someone who is looking for a DJ.

Shortly after that, I met a lovely young man from India who is a graphic designer. His girlfriend is also here from India. He offered to do the book cover for this Uber Diary. I may take him up on that—but I'm not sure yet. Students are so helpful and they are very willing to help you if you have a problem, especially with your cell phone or computer, and they have no problem with giving you their opinion or advice.

# NCA Cheerleader

Today I met a lovely young girl from England who is staying here to do Cheerleading. She is a Level Five International Champion with the "Great White Sharks". Her family must be very proud of her. She hopes to teach Cheerleading some day. I'm sure she will make a great coach. She speaks with so much passion for it.

# Thank You For The Birthday Wishes

I met two lovely young girls from India today again. I was taking them to their job. During our conversation, I mentioned I was going out for dinner with my husband that night. They asked if it was for a special occasion.

"It's my birthday," I replied.

Our conversation was very pleasant and at the end of their trip, they handed me a piece of folded paper. This is what it said,

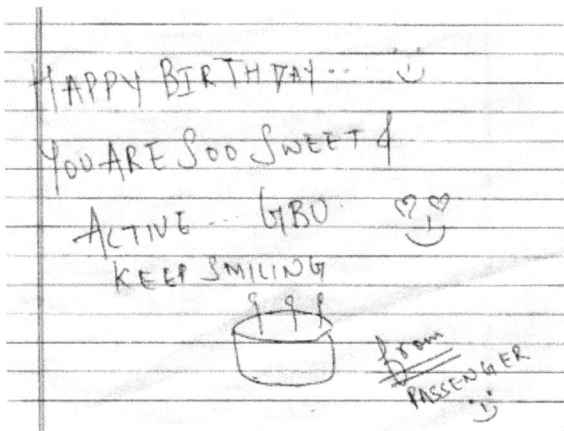

"Thank you, girls, this means a lot." I said. I still have it to this day.

# A Fun Afternoon With Two Entrepreneurs

Today I picked up two young student entrepreneurs. One was in his 20s and the other in his early 30s. They both were taking business courses and they both were born here. One worked for a company that sold furnaces and the other for a company that installed solar power panels.

They requested that I wait for them after the first stop and to continue on with them to their final destination. I certainly didn't mind waiting. They were so appreciative, polite and full of humour. They were doing business on their phone and I could tell that they had the talent to be entrepreneurs just by the way they did their business. The one young man seemed to have the gift of gab. He was very articulate and polite, and I think he will be a very good salesman. They were fun and funny, and they joked the entire drive to their destination. We even stopped at one point along the way to grab a coffee, and I was on the receiving end of a medium.

Thanks again to my passengers for the coffee, laughs and great conversation. It made my day.

# Basketball???

I picked up a nice young man from out of town. I think he was coming here from out West. He said that he was the owner of a basketball team and that he was here on business. I am not a sports person, so I wouldn't know enough about basketball to keep up the conversation. But he told me that his fiancé is joining him here and they are getting married in the summer. When I dropped him off at his destination I congratulated him on his up and coming wedding.

The next pickup was a young student from India who is here studying engineering. It's his first winter in Canada, and he misses his family back home—especially his mother.
"Now I have to cook for myself and I'm not very good at it! My mother would always do this for me," he said.

*India, officially the Republic of India is a country in South Asia. It is the seventh-largest country by area, the second-most populous country (with over 1.2 billion people).*

# Serenading

Today I picked up a gentleman who told me he is a singer and that he was in New York cutting a CD. He told me he was also an actor, a professor, and runs a School of Music. Wow! A man of many hats. I told him that I was a poet.

"Oh?" He said, "You get it then,"

"Oh yes, I do". I replied.

This gentleman is very talented. He even sang a few of his songs, which I appreciated very much. He enjoyed the cabaret style of music, and he has appeared in several familiar shows. I felt very privileged to be in his presence.

When you are an Uber driver, you never know who your passenger could be!

# Meeting New Friends

Today I picked up a young gentleman from East Africa. His father has his own electrical company there. I asked him if he was going to be working for his father's business? He said he wasn't sure and that he may start his own electrical business here in Canada. He then told me a little about his home. He said he lived near the highest mountain in Tanzania. He said the only snow he sees is on the top of the mountain. It sounded beautiful.

*Tanzania officially the United Republic of Tanzania: a sovereign state in eastern Africa within the African Great Lakes region. It borders Kenya and Uganda to the north; Rwanda, Burundi, and the Democratic Republic of the Congo to the west; Zambia, Malawi, and Mozambique to the south; and the Indian Ocean to the east.*

# Future Vet

Met a young girl today, who was going to a stable to ride her horse. She loves horses and her dream is to become a vet. Her passion shows on her face when she talks about her horse. I truly think she will make a wonderful vet.

Most of my passengers are from the Tri-City area. The Tri-Cities, also known as Kitchener-Cambridge-Waterloo, is a metropolitan area located in Southern Ontario, Canada. These cities, as well as surrounding rural municipalities, collectively make up the Regional Municipality of Waterloo. The census metropolitan area had a population of 523,894 in 2016, making it the fourth largest metropolitan area in Ontario, after Toronto, Ottawa and Hamilton, and the tenth largest metropolitan area in the country.

The Tri-City area is known for its high concentration of information technology companies—leading it to be frequently characterized as "Canada's Silicon Valley".

The Tri-Cities are also University towns with a large student population from the University of Waterloo, Wilfrid Laurier University, and Conestoga College. The area is also known for its high concentration of Mennonites. There are many Mennonite churches in the area, serving the New Mennonites, Conservative Mennonites, Old Order Mennonite and the Mennonite Brethren.

# Addictions

I picked up a mom today, and I noticed she had some clothing in a plastic bag.

"Hi, how are you today?" I asked.

"I'm OK," she said, "I'm booking myself into rehab. I'm addicted to Meth and alcohol."

"Wow! Congratulations on taking that BIG step", I replied.

"Thanks, I'm getting tired of putting my family through hell,"

She then proceeded to tell me that she has two grown children and a husband.

"My husband has been there for me from the start, and he is the one who has always taken me to get help, but I keep falling backwards," she said. "This time, I'm doing it on my own. I made the call."

"You did the right thing, I hope it goes well for you," I replied.

I dropped her off at the facility. As I retrieved her belongings and gave them to her, I asked if it would be OK if I hugged her. She seemed surprised, but eventually smiled and said, "yes,"

I gave her a hug and wished her luck. I watched her go through the doors and said a silent prayer that she would make it this time. There are many treatment centers in the KW area for those who need it, you just need to look them up.

# Identity Theft With A Twist

I was called to another city and picked up a beautiful young student who had lived there all her life. I picked her up from her job. She said she was going to her second job.

"It must be difficult having two jobs and going to college as well. When do you get time for yourself?" I asked.

"Oh, I don't," she replied.

I was impressed. "You must be very determined," I said.

"Actually, I just applied for a student loan and found out that I'm in debt," she replied. "My identity was stolen,"

"Oh, My God. I'm so sorry! Are the police involved?" I asked.

"Oh yes," she said. "They found the person responsible,"

"That's great," I replied.

"That's not the worst of it," she spoke again, "it was my own family member. You see, there's an issue with drugs and alcohol in my family, which is why all my money has disappeared." She went on, "I'm in debt for thousands of dollars, that's why I have to work two jobs now. My family member has been charged and I don't think I will ever get any of it back."

I sat in her driveway with the car turned off and continued to listen to her story. She desperately needed to talk to someone. I couldn't offer her any advice, but I could offer her my ear and empathy. We sat for quite a while, and eventually, she apologized for taking up all my time.

"It's truly OK," I said.

"Well, I must go", she spoke again, "thanks so much for listening."

I wished her luck with everything.

"Thank you," she replied.

"I feel so much better just getting this out."
"You're very welcome," I said.
I still think about her.

# Meeting New Friends Part 2

Today I met a young student from Nigeria—the southern part of the Delta state.

"It's one of the oil producing countries," she said, "and my tribe is Urhobo."

She is here to do her masters in Innovation and Entrepreneurship. She is a very smart young lady and it was a pleasure meeting her.

*The Federal Republic of Nigeria: (commonly referred to as Nigeria), is a federal republic in West Africa, bordering Benin in the west, Chad and Cameroon in the east, and Niger in the north. Its coast in the south lies on the Gulf of Guinea in the Atlantic Ocean. It comprises 36 states and the Federal Capital Territory, where the capital, Abuja is located. Nigeria is officially a democratic secular country*

# Meeting New Friends Part 3

Today I met a father of two awesome young children—a daughter and a son. I immediately noticed how well behaved they were. They seemed to be very happy and polite young children. They even thanked me for the treats I offered them. I always try to keep little treats for children as well as my adult passengers, along with bottles of water.

Shortly after that, I picked up a young man from work. He has been working there for a couple of years and enjoys his job. He takes Uber home every day. He doesn't drive, and he finds Uber a lot cheaper than a taxi. I pick him up quite often, and he tells me about his family and co-workers. I find my passengers become very comfortable with me quickly because I like to talk to them, which is why they often share stories about themselves.

I also picked up four students going to work right from school that day. They normally get the bus and ride it for the long one-hour drive to work the night shift, and then take the long bus ride back home again. These students were here from India. They said they usually sleep on the bus ride back, then get ready for their classes. They needed to do that to pay for their education. Now that is dedication!

# All Dressed Up

Today I got a call to pick up a couple at a local motel, and as I pulled up toward the entrance, I noticed a taxi parked in front of me and a well-dressed gentleman talking to him.

I waited for my passenger to come. The gentleman that was talking to the taxi came towards me,

"Margaret?" He asked.

I acknowledged him and then he and his wife got into my car.

"I'm so angry," he said. "We ordered a taxi but it didn't come for over an hour, so we had to order an Uber. We have to be at our friend's wedding and now we are going to be late!" He spoke. "The taxi just arrived when you came. I had to tell him to never-mind and that I hired an Uber."

"I'm sorry to hear that," I replied, "and what time is the wedding?"

"In fifteen minutes," he said.

"I will try my best to get you there without you being too late," I assured him.

Long story short, I got them there on time and they weren't late. They were very happy and appreciative, and I didn't speed—a lot. Lol.

# Blessed To Live In Canada

My second call today was to pick up a young student who wanted to go to Toronto to visit with her long-time friend. As we drove and talked, she mentioned that she was gay. She then waited for my reaction before continuing.

"In my country, people who are gay are not accepted," she said, "and they may even be put in prison."

"Well, it's more accepted here in Canada," I replied, "but I'm sure you'll always get someone who won't agree. Me personally, I accept people for who they are regardless of their sexuality."

She became very comfortable with me, and confided in me that she was worried that some of the students in her class from her country might ostracize her if they found out. It was sad to hear. Especially since she was here in Canada, because on one hand, it was great to be here in this lovely country where you can be whatever you want to be. But on the other, if your fellow classmates are from your country and found out you were gay, that they may continue ostracize you. She shouldn't have to worry about that here—not in Canada. I asked her how her family felt about it? She told me that they had to seek counseling to learn what being gay was, but they were very supportive.

"That's great, at least your family will be there for you and you don't have to hide it from them," I stated.

She agreed. I hope things become easier for her in the future. I hope she hangs in there!

# Final Thoughts

My experience as an Uber Driver has definitely increased my faith in the youth of today. The young students of today will benefit our country tremendously. When they finish their education, we will have people from all walks of life sharing their knowledge and experience with our city and country.

I have met future Doctors, Lawyers, Engineers, Musicians, Personal Support Workers, Veterinarians, Nurses, Councilors and so on. Everyone I've met and talked to spoke highly of Canada, and they felt very blessed to be here—to have the opportunities that are available to them.

In my two years of driving for Uber, I met some awesome people. I have even shared a little of myself with them, as they did with me. I have also been educated. I have gotten the opportunity to learn about other countries, cultures and more.

Uber has grown substantially in our city now. Also, the age factor seems to be changing. When I first started driving it was just the young students that were primarily using Uber, Now I have businessmen, entrepreneurs and older passengers, both male and female. I also found out that people are basically the same no matter where they are from. They have a family they love, and they miss them. I also learned that many students struggle. Especially the foreign stydents, because they arrive in a new country leaving their loved ones behind, trying to adjust to our culture and laws, but they are still happy to go through it all just to get the chance at an education and a better life.

Last, I have learned to be a better and more confident driver through these experiences, and I will continue to be an Uber Driver until I can no longer drive. I also encourage other seniors to get out there and give it a try. What do you have to lose?

# All Your Comments

I do read and love your feedback and comments. It makes my day. It encourages me to keep going, and if I have made a difference in just one person's life by listening, by showing them that someone cares, or just by getting them to their destination easier, then that's enough for me. I want each of my passengers to know that you have given meaning to this old Great Granny's Life. Thank You So Much.

# Rider Comments

May 2016 - "You were awesome!"
June 2016 - "Such a sweetheart,"
July 2016 - "She was wonderful,"
July 2016 - "Wonderful driver,"
August 2016 - "Thank you so much Margaret, it was nice meeting you!"
August 2016 - "Good conversation."
August 2016 - "That was fun!"
August 2016 - "You are a lovely human being and you made me feel less homesick."
August 2016 - "Awesome trip!"
August 2016 - "Great asset to the Uber family!"
August 2016 - "A real treat!"
August 2016 - "Thank you for getting us safely to our destination, it was a pleasure riding with you."
September 2016 - "This was the best part of my morning. So, thank you, I couldn't have asked for a better drive!"
September 2016 - "She was a fun and sweet driver,"
September 2016 - "Very friendly,"
October 2016 - "Gave me a free bottle of water!"
October 2016 - "Thanks!"
October 2016 - "Thanks for the pleasant ride."
October 2016 - "Thank you"
October 2016 - "Everything went well. Thank You!"
October 2016 - "Thank you,"
December 2016 - "Margaret was splendid, personable and provided legit life coaching—Loved her!"

## Margaret High

December 2016 - "Super sweet, cutest little lady ever! Thank you."
December 2016 - "Thanks, and Merry Christmas!"
December 2016 - "So cute!"
January 2017 - "Thank you for my first Uber ride, Ma'am."
January 2017 - "Thank you so much"
January 2017 - "Had a great conversation and a comfortable ride. Very much appreciated the bottle of water."
January 2017 - "Thank you so much for the awesome drive! Great chatting with you!"
January 2017 - "What a sweet lady. She was excellent! So nice, and made great conversation. Made me feel comfortable."
February 2017 - "Most favourite Uber driver!"
February 2017 - "Thank You,"
March 2017 - "Thanks, Margaret! Was a pleasure"
March 2017 - "Thanks Margaret You're a real G-Thang!"
March 2017 - "Thank You."
March 2017 - "Keep up the great work!"
April 2017 - "Cooperative and friendly!"
April 2017 - "Very friendly."
April 2017 - "Such a pleasant lady to talk to."
April 2017 - "Thank You."
May 2017 - "Hope you had a great lunch..."
May. 2017 - "Best driver by far! Very kind and great conversation. Thank You!"
May 2017 - "Thanks for being so lovely."
May 2017 - "Thank you!"
June 2017 - "Super Lady,"
August 2017 - "Excellent!"
August 2017 - "Very friendly and fast!"
August 2017 - "Lovely conversation and a very welcoming manner. Thank You! Great driver!"
September 2017 - "Thank you very much!"
August 2017 - "Beast!"
October 2017 - "One of the best Uber drivers I've had the pleasure of meeting,"
October 2017 - "Great driver and a nice person,"
November 2017 - "Thanks for the advice about the Tiger store,"

# Great Granny Margaret's Uber Diary

December 2017 - "Thank you so much! You were great, I loved talking to you and all that you told me about your experience and being the younger you. You have inspired me so much! I got so motivated after I heard the things you are doing with your life. You are awesome!"

January 2018 - "Thank you so much, you lifted my spirits!"

January 2018 - "Consummate, professional, charming and amicable!"

January 2018 - "My first Uber driver in Canada, thank you so much for making It a wonderful experience for me!"

February 2018 - "The best Uber driver I ever had! So awesome! Thank you!" :)

January 2018 - "Thank you for the great conversation. Hoping to have a ride with you again soon!"

February 2018 - "You just made my day, hope to travel with you again soon."

April 2018 - "I wish I could add others as well. It was a great conversation. Expert navigation, neat and tidy, great amenities and above and beyond service."

April 2018 - "It was a very good conversation. I hope to see a lot more Uber drivers like you! Nice meeting you, have a Blessing day."

May 2018 - "Great service and excellent conversation ten out of ten score!"

May 2018 - "One of the best Uber drivers. She is always cheerful."

June 2018 - "Margaret you were very sweet and made me feel a lot better this morning. Thank you for the ride!"

June 2018 - "Good Luck with your book!!"

## Acknowledgments

First, I would like to thank my son for his suggestion to be an Uber Driver. I would also like to thank my husband and the rest of my family for their continuous support. And a special thanks goes out to my passengers for all their kind words and encouragement. You all have made a tremendous impact on my life. I loved listening to each of your stories, your hopes, and your dreams for the future. You've shared with me things about your family, your homeland, struggles, and passions. I think we as Canadians, often take things for granted—most of all our education system, and yet, people come from all around the world just to get the many options and opportunities that are offered right here in our own backyard.

Some of the people I pick up have one, two, or more jobs to help cover the cost of their education, along with financial help from their parents back home. I definitely have a new respect for students. Good luck to you all and thank you again!

www.ingramcontent.com/pod-product-compliance
Lightning Source LLC
Chambersburg PA
CBHW052031290426
44112CB00014B/2464